& WATER
RESISTANT

AFN

WATERPROOF

Pocket Guide No.1

Richard Rule's

Flyfishing Lakes

• What fly to use!
• Tactics!

REVISED EDITION
Now in 2nd reprint by popular demand!

by Richard Rule
with Rick Keam
and Bill Classon

CONTENTS

Richard Rule's

Flyfishing Lakes

by Richard Rule
with Rick Keam
and Bill Classon

Front Cover Illustration - Based upon David Ashcroft's painting 'Brook Trout on Clarence Lagoon'

Illustrations - Phill Jones

Knots - Geoff Wilson

Design & Production - Dennis Keys

Publishers Bill & Helen Classon

SECTION ONE

TACKLE

RODS & LINES

A moderately fast action 8′6″ or 9′ (2.6–2.7 m) for a 6 or 7 weight line is ideal.

Floating lines are the preferred choice in most situations-deeper water can be searched with wet flies using longer leaders. There are circumstances where a spare spool with a sink-tip, or a sinking line and short leader will pay off.

LEADERS

KNOTLESS TAPERED LEADER: These are available in a variety of lengths and tippet thickness.

COMPOUND: Different fishing conditions and changing situations sometimes require features unobtainable in commercial leaders. Many anglers make up 'compound' or customised leaders from monofilament of varying diameters and lengths.

MATCHING LEADERS TO FLIES

Your leader and tippet should suit both your fly line and the size of flies you plan to use.

	BUTT DIAM (In.)	TIP DIAM (In.)	SIZE	HOOK
10lb.	.026	.011	0X	1/0-6
9lb.	.022	.010	1X	2-6
7lb.	.022	.009	2X	2-6
6lb.	.022	.008	3X	4-10
5lb.	.022	.007	4X	6-14
4lb.	.022	.006	5X	10-18
3lb.	.020	.005	6X	14-22

COMPOUND LEADERS

11 ft (3.3 m) Dry Fly Leader - Calm Conditions

Diameter	.023″ (.58 mm)	.019″ (.48 mm)	.015″ (.38mm)	.011″ (.28 mm)	.007″ (.18 mm)	.006″ (.15 mm)
Length	40″ (100 cm)	13″ (33 cm)	13″ (33 cm)	13″ (33 cm)	12″ (30 cm)	40″ (100 cm)

9 ft (2.5 m) Wet Fly or Dry Fly in Stiff Breeze

Diameter	.023″ (.58 mm)	.019″ (.48 mm)	.015″ (.38 mm)	.011″ (.28 mm)	.007″ (.18 mm)
Length	40″ (100 cm)	13″ (33 cm)	13″ (33 cm)	13″ (33 cm)	20″ (50 cm)

10 ft (2.99 m) All Purpose Leader

Diameter	.023″ (.58 mm)	.019″ (.48 mm)	.015″ (.38 mm)	.011″ (.28 mm)	.007″ (.18 mm)
Length	40″ (100 cm)	13″ (33 cm)	13″ (33 cm)	13″ (33 cm)	40″ (100 cm)

KNOTS & RIGS

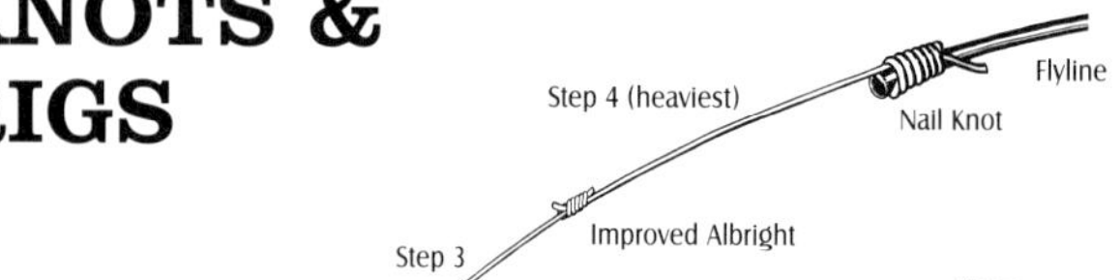

For further information on knots consult Geoff Wilson's Complete Book of Fishing Knots and Rigs.

ATTACHING FLIES TO LEADER

Locked Half Blood Knot

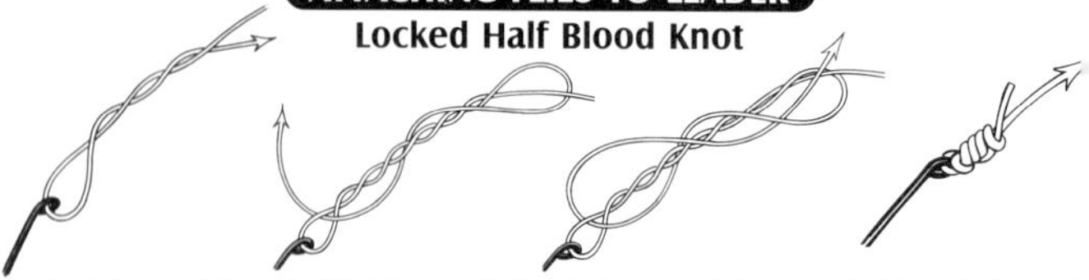

1. Thread the eye of the hook and wind the tag back around the main line four or five times.
2. Wind the tag back around the knot and through the eye of the first wrap of line around the eye of the hook.
3. Now thread the tag back through the loop at the top of the knot. This locks the knot so it can't slip.
4. Tighten the knot with gentle pressure on the tippet.

Improved Turle Knot

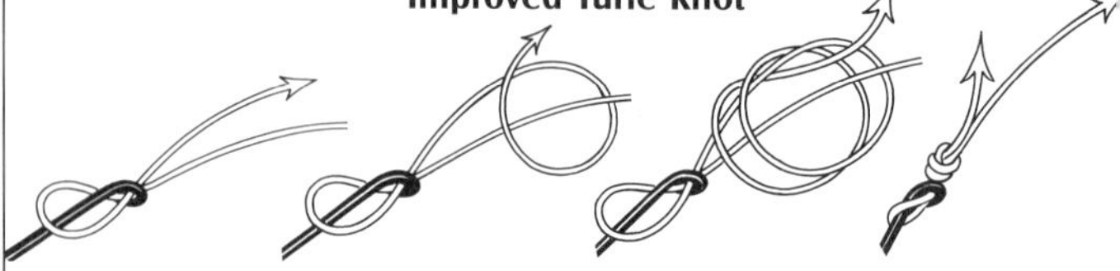

1. Thread the line through hook eye, take the line around the head of the fly and back through the eye of the hook again.
2. Encircle the standing part of the tippet with the tag.
3. And again, making two turns in all, then pass the tag over, and back through the centre of those two turns.
4. Close up the knot with gentle pressure on the tag and slide the knot right down into the eye of the hook.

ATTACHING FLYLINE TO LEADER

Nail Knot

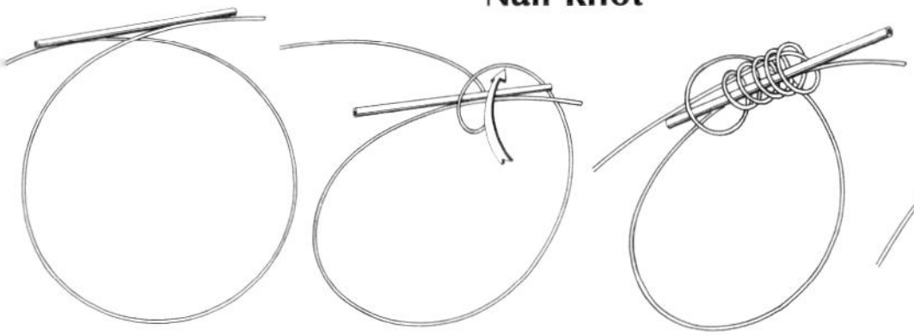

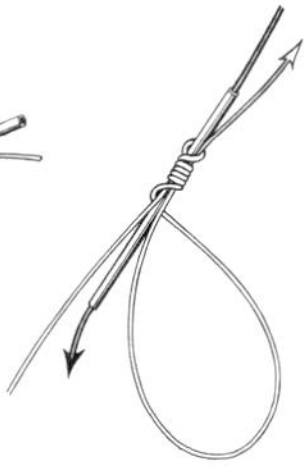

1. Make a loop in the backing or leader and lay the metal tube alongside the cross-over.

2. Begin wrapping the tube with the backing or leader.

3. Make at least six wraps.

4. Close the knot up tight on the tube and insert the fly line into the tube.

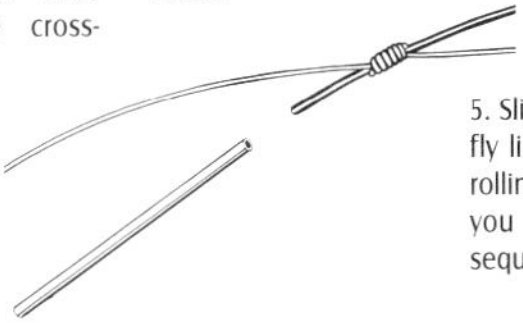

5. Slide the knot off the tube, onto the fly line, and close the knot up gently, rolling it between thumb and finger as you do so to keep the wraps in sequence.

JOINING LEADER SECTIONS

Improved Albright Knot

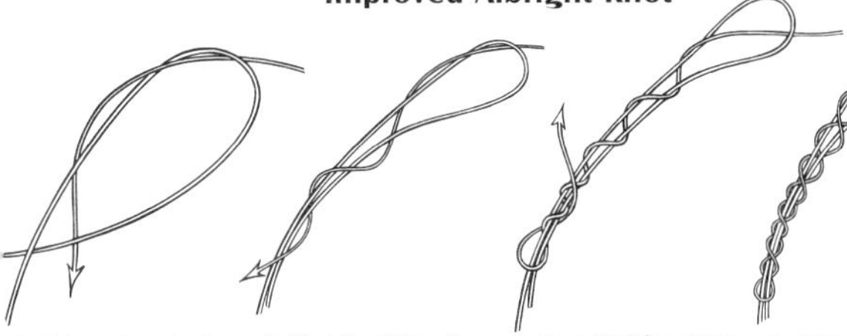

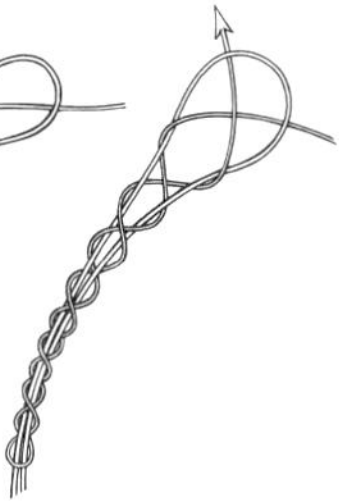

1. Make a loop in the heavier line and pass the lighter line through the loop.

2. Bind the lighter line around the loop of heavier line five times.

3. Then bind five times back in the opposite direction.

4. Here we have five wraps of line one direction around the loop and five in the opposite direction.

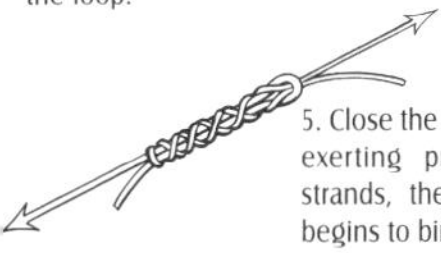

5. Close the knot up gently, first by exerting pressure on all four strands, then – when the knot begins to bind – release both tags and tension the knot as shown.

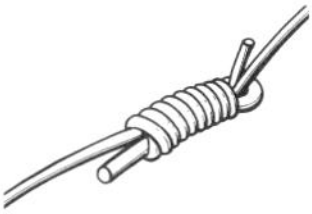

6. The finished knot should look like this.

SECTION TWO

COMMON RETRIEVES:

GIVING LIFE TO THE FLY

The retrieval methods outlined below are suitable from both the lake bank or in a boat.

1. BASIC STRIP RETRIEVE

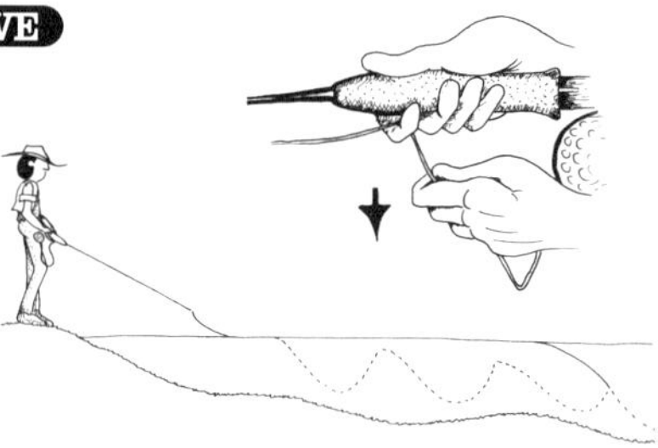

Floating/Sinking/Sinktip lines

Place the line between your thumb and first finger of the rod hand. With the other hand, retrieve the line in a series of strips and pauses. The length and speed of the strip depends entirely on the type of trout food you want to suggest.

2. FIGURE-8 & HAND-TWIST RETRIEVES

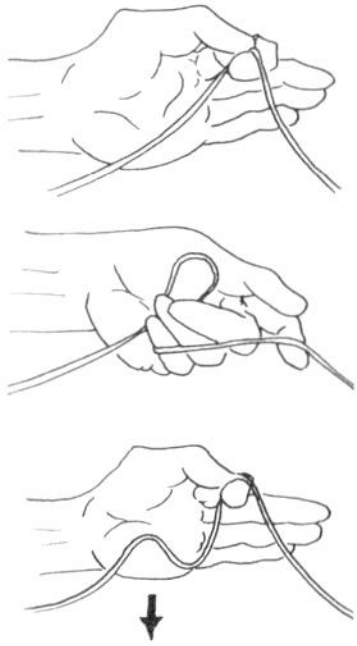

Floating/Sinking/Sinktip lines

This is a technique that will suggest slower, shorter and more hesitant movements. In the Figure-8 technique, the thumb and little finger act as two posts between which the line is woven in a Figure-8 pattern, either smoothly or with a jerky rotation of the wrist. In the Hand-Twist Retrieve, the line is grasped between thumb and index finger, then the remaining fingers extend to draw back 5 to 8 cm of line, which begins to loop around the bottom of the little finger. With an inward rotation of the wrist, the loop is extended over the back of the fingers to the thumb, which traps it against the forefinger to form a teardrop shape. The bottom three fingers are then withdrawn from this loop and the process continued.

3. SINK & RISE

Floating/Sinktip lines

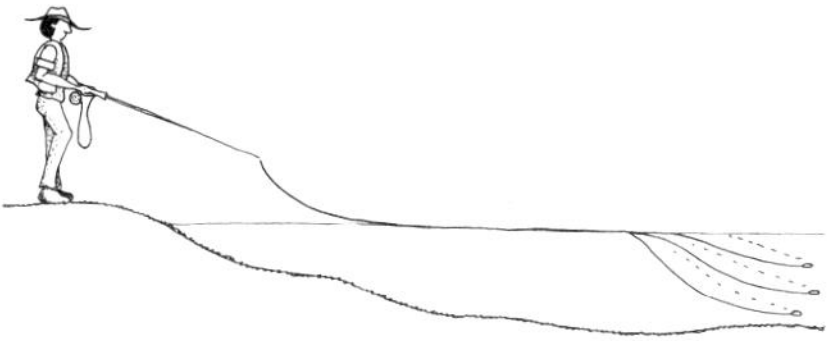

Cast out a wet fly on a floating or sinktip line, allowing it to sink to the required depth. Use a slow, steady strip retrieve to bring the fly to the surface to suggest emerging insects. You can repeat it a number of times before re-casting.

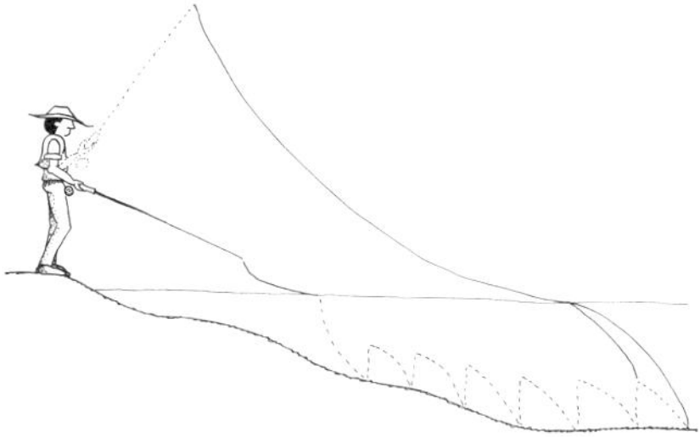

Alternatively, keep a tight line and draw the fly to the surface by lifting the rod tip slowly and steadily from horizontal. This method can be deadly during midge emergences and can also be used to suggest rising nymphs that return to the bottom, or water boatmen repeatedly rising to the surface for air.

4. HAYES BOAT-DRIFTING RETRIEVE

Floating/Sinking/Sinktip lines

When a number of anglers are in the boat this method should allow everyone to fish in safety. A roll cast is made to get the line out and the fly allowed to sink to the required depth. Commence a steady retrieve or draw to swim the fly back up to the surface. Once the line has been retrieved, the technique is repeated.

SECTION THREE

FEATURES TO FISH

Successful lake flyfishers concentrate their efforts in and around lake margins. These areas sustain a consistent, easily obtained, concentration of food for trout. Newcomers often think that the deeper the water the bigger and more numerous the fish will be, but the reverse is more often true. Anglers who regularly wade right out to present prodigious casts have often unknowingly passed through the most productive waters in the lake.

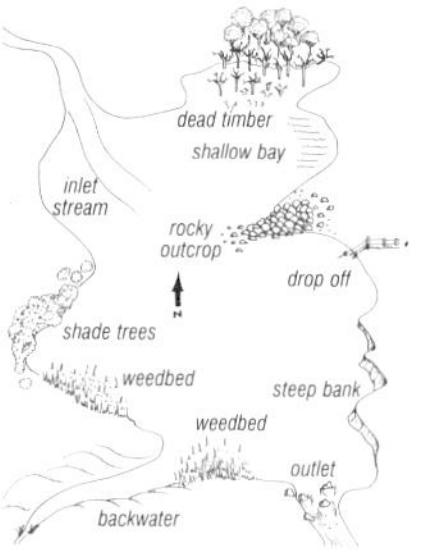

WEEDBEDS

Most stable lakes have numerous food rich weedbeds close to the shoreline where nymphs caddis, mayfly, midge, dragon and damselflies, snails, tadpoles, and small baitfish live.

The most productive beds are found in sheltered bays along gently sloping banks running into water that is knee to waist deep.

Off shore weedbeds, not immediately visible, may be detected by scouting along the bank for clumps of washed up vegetation.

FISHING TECHNIQUES FOR WEEDBEDS

1. To avoid being continually snagged it is best to fish over and around weedbeds rather than through them.

2. In deeper water use the countdown method to determine the depth of the weeds. To do this count the seconds that it takes the fly to sink to the bottom. If for example, it settles in weed after sinking for 19 seconds, then begin your future retrieves at 17 seconds to keep the fly just over the vegetation.

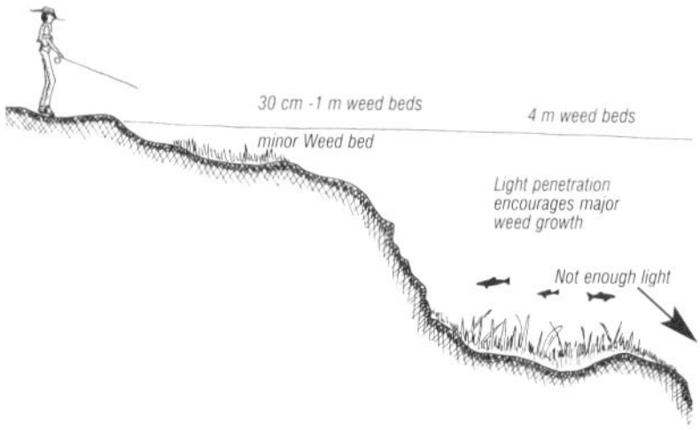

ROCKY OUTCROPS

Often these areas extend for a surprising distance out into deeper water and are home to yabbies, smelt, dragonfly larvae ('mudeyes') and certain mayfly nymphs.

FISHING TECHNIQUES FOR OUTCROPS

1. In water less than 2m deep a floating line with a 3-5m leader is adequate. Fish a wet fly thoroughly around the boulders with a slow figure-8 or hand twist retrieve.

2. Water more than 2m deep is best fished with a sinktip line, full sinking line or sinking leader.

LOG JAMS & DROWNED TIMBER

Log jams are piles of dead timber that accumulate mainly along windward shores. These areas form prime feeding locations, due to high concentrations of nymphs, minnows, yabbies and mudeyes.

FISHING TECHNIQUES FOR LOG JAMS

1. Fish these areas in the low light conditions of dawn, dusk, overcast drizzly days and at night.

2. Keep casts short and manageable: a maximum of 10 metres is normally sufficient. Use a shortened leader down to a 3–4 kg tippet to combat the innumerable snags.

3. If the water is not too deep try wading in and fishing your fly from different positions around the trees and logs.

INFLOWS & RIVER MOUTHS

Inflowing streams generally provide oxygenated, cool, food-rich water. Trout will position themselves at the river mouth alongside the main current particularly at dawn, dusk and on overcast days. Beetles, nymphs and nondescript search patterns are always good fly options.

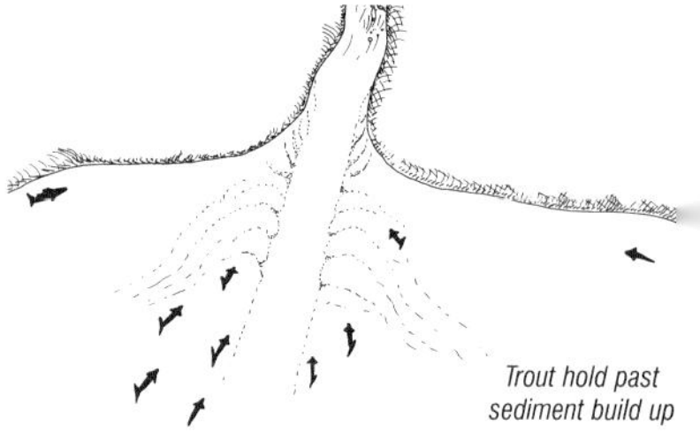

FISHING TECHNIQUES FOR INFLOWS

1. Using a sinking leader or sink-tip line, cast a matuka or smelt pattern upstream, then let it drift back into the calmer water and commence a strip retrieve.

2. Use a floating line, 2.7-3.6 metre leader. Take up a position off to the side of the inflowing current and fish your pattern on the surface or tumbled along the bottom.

SUNKEN RIVER BEDS/CHANNELS

Channels and sunken river beds, if visible, normally appear as dark serpentine stretches of water wandering through the body of a lake. In dams, stands of dead trees may also give an indication of where the old river course is. In warm conditions in shallower lakes, trout will often congregate in the deeper, cooler water that these channels provide.

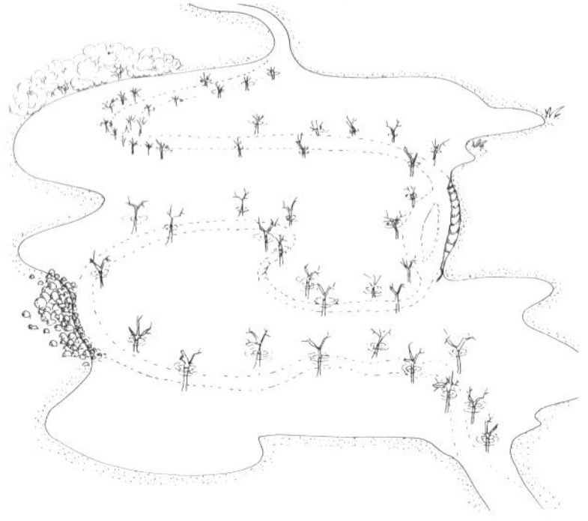

FISHING TECHNIQUES FOR CHANNELS

1. If fishing 'blind' try casting a sinking line across the channel letting the fly sink to the bottom and use a Figure-8 or a jerky stop/start retrieve. Strikes often occur as the fly moves out of the channel.

DROP-OFFS

Drop-offs, signified by darker water, are found where shallow water falls away rapidly into the depths and are commonly cruised by trout which feel safe knowing that deeper water is close. Waters that are heavily fished during the day often force trout to stay out around these demarcation zones until darkness encourages them into the shallows to feed.

TIP: If fish are being easily spooked in the shallows, try rubbing mud on the leader to dull the finish.

FISHING TECHNIQUES FOR DROP OFFS

1. Cast your fly out into the deeper water on a floating or sinking line, let the imitation settle on the bottom and then instigate a slow Figure-8 or Hand-Twist retrieve.

FLOOD PLAINS & BACKWATERS

When water levels rise, trout will move into the shallows to feed on worms, beetles and other drowned terrestrials.

Early morning and dusk are normally the best time of day, but trout may move in at any time, especially if it is overcast or windy.

FISHING TECHNIQUES FOR BACKWATERS

1. Use a floating line to search the water with beetle patterns or general-purpose standbys like Sloane's Fur Fly, Yeti, Mrs Simpson, Wigram's Robin or various matukas. In discoloured water, black and green are the most visible colours.

2. Prospecting with these flies in deeper water with a sinking line is sometimes effective, particularly if brighter conditions mean the fish are likely to be further offshore.

SECTION FOUR

TECHNIQUES TO FISH THE WATER

POLARISING

Polarising is best done on fine sunny cloudless days between 10 am and 4 pm when the sun is high. Don't look for trout, look for shadows or shapes. Have the sun behind you irrespective of wind direction.

POLARISING METHODS

1. Use a floating line, 2.7-4.6m leader down to a 5x,6x tippet. If using small wets or nymphs, grease the leader to within 30 cm of the fly.

2. Train yourself to scan the water 5-10 metres in front. It is rare to actually see the trout clearly so learn to look for subtle signs of trout.

3. Have enough fly line off the reel to minimise false casting and be quick because trout are usually 'one cast only' fish when in shallow water.

4. If a trout approaches your fly, resist striking until you either see the 'wink under water' as the fish opens and closes its mouth, or movement of the leader at the point where it enters the water. Don't be over zealous when striking because tippets are usually very fine.

5. The 'jumping nymph' technique is a useful presentation if casting to a fish feeding off the bottom. The first step is to cast out the fly and let it sink completely. As the fish approaches to within 1–2 metres of the fly, give the rod tip a gentle twitch to 'jump' the nymph off the bottom to draw a strike.

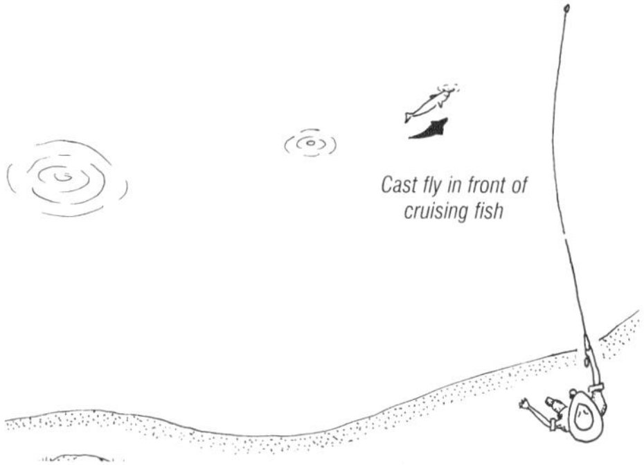

BLIND FISHING WINDWARD SHORES

Fishing with the wind at your back is easier, but generally less productive than fishing a shore parallel to the wind or into which the wind is blowing. The reason is that trout will be feeding on the stirred-up morsels under the cover of choppy water along these windward shores.

TECHNIQUES TO CONSIDER WHEN BLIND FISHING IN THE WIND

1. On shores parallel to the wind, concentrate on areas where the calmer and clearer margins meet discoloured wind-blown water.

2. On shores facing into the wind, wade out a short way and fish along the wave lines, or wade well out and fish back along the shoreline.

3. A lack of line control and wind knots may result from long casting. Keep your game short.

4. Good searching patterns include Mrs Simpson, Sloane's Fur Fly, Yeti, Wigram's Robin, various matukas, large nymphs in brown, black or green, Fuzzy Wuzzy, Hamill's Killer or Tom Jones. Traditional wet flies like Watson's Fancy, Peter Ross and Alexandra are well worth a try.

NIGHT FISHING

Preparation is essential

- First make a detailed mental map of the terrain to help you to find your way around in the dark.
- Clues to look for may include mudeye shucks on bankside trees or foliage, yabby holes along the bank or snails in amongst the aquatic vegetation.
- The biggest fish in the lake generally feed at night so it pays to use tippets in the 3–4 kg range and thoroughly check all your knots.
- Check the batteries in your torch.

• An ideal scenario would be a partly cloudy sky, modest ripple on the water and a rising barometer.

• The period between dusk and full darkness often sees many trout become temporarily less active whilst they attain their night vision.

• It is also thought that brown trout can require as much as two hours of full darkness before they actively feed again.

TECHNIQUES FOR NIGHT FISHING

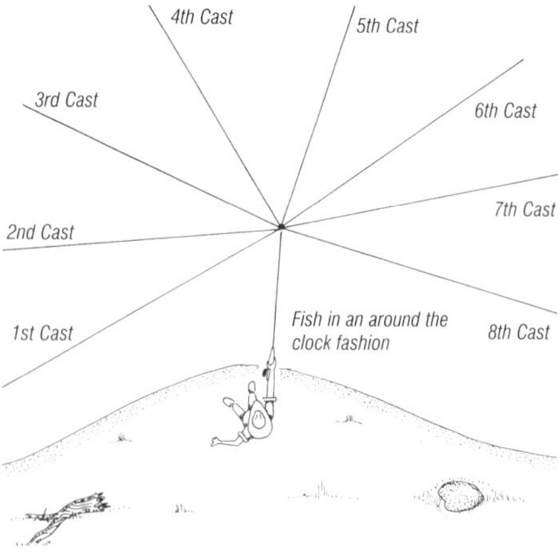

1. When fishing the last part of the day, wade out into deeper water to target the trout that are preparing to migrate into the shallows.

2. To take advantage of the last rays of light, cast into the setting sun. Use repetitive cast in a round the clock fashion.

3. In the darkness your hearing is important to locating trout.

4. Bulky flies are commonly used at night because they displace water and their pulsating action is easily detected by trout. Flies like a Black Muddler, Marabou Muddler (fished slowly and jerkily at or near the surface), Black Woolly Bugger, Craig's Night-time, Black or Black & Red Matuka,Wigram's Robin or a large Alexandra. If the water is extremely cold, try slowing the retrieve so the fly is barely moving. Use short leaders.

5. Dry flies can also be productive, particularly if you are matching insect species that hatch during the night. Getting your line of vision down as close as possible to the water surface can help you see the fly.

6. If you are failing to get a solid hookup, try holding the rod tip at a 45° angle. The small section of slack line may remedy the problem of 'short takers' and allow timid trout to hook themselves.

FLYFISHING FROM A BOAT

- Minimise noise by putting hessian bags or similar soundproofing material across the floor.
- If rowing use teflon rowlocks or smear rowlocks with fly floatant.
- Use your electric motor.

1. If two or more people are in the boat, be mindful of your partner. To avoid mid air backcast tangles, cast parallel to each other. Establishing an imaginary dividing line across the middle of the boat may be useful.

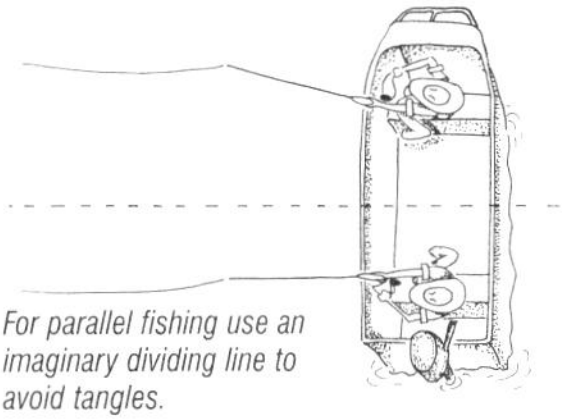

For parallel fishing use an imaginary dividing line to avoid tangles.

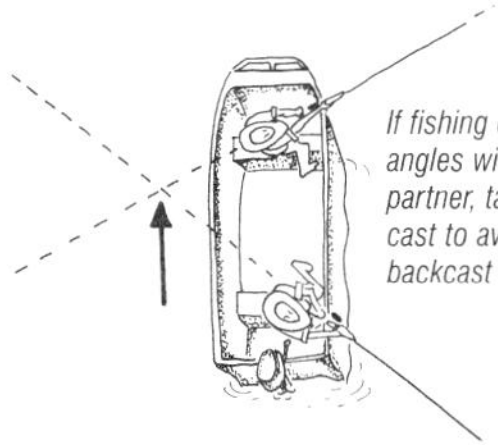

If fishing on diagonal angles with your partner, take turns to cast to avoid backcast tangles.

2. Keep your back casts high, particularly if it is windy, and strip in slack line before you lift the fly to recast. Doing this will avoid throwing low trajectory back casts across the boat and possibly into your partner.

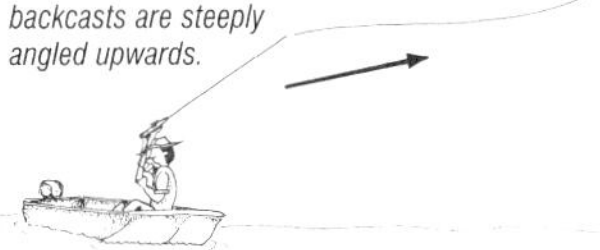

For the safety of others in the boat ensure backcasts are steeply angled upwards.

3. If your companion is rowing, keep track of where the oars are. Let him or her know when and where you plan to cast next.

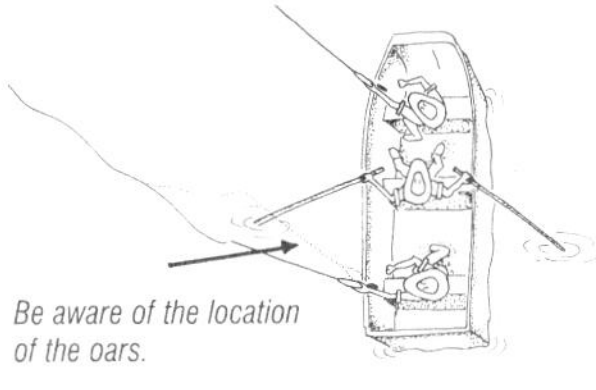

Be aware of the location of the oars.

4. Hooked fish can often run straight back and under your boat, so be prepared to strip in line quickly, and the rower lifting the oars out of the way.

Avoid the oars whilst angling a fish the oarsman should pull up the oars to keep the water clear.

DRIFT-FISHING WINDLANES

• Windlanes appear as distinctive strips of calm water on an otherwise breeze-rippled lake surface.

• Food tends to collect in such areas creating prime feeding locations for trout, particularly rainbows.

• Lanes formed by prevailing winds will appear in the same places from day to day and generally provide the most productive fishing.

TECHNIQUES FOR DRIFT FISHING WINDLANES.

1. Position your vessel parallel to the windlane and drift down with the breeze. Use oars or an electric outboard to keep near the windlane if necessary.

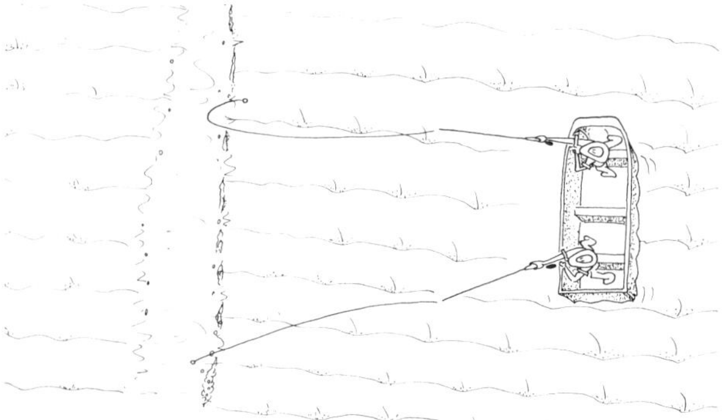

2. A collapsible parachute drogue allows you to drift slowly if the breeze is fresh.

3. Once you have reached the end of the windlane, it often pays to move back up to the start and drift down again. Try to polarise the water in front of you.

4. Fly choice is largely dictated by what the trout are feeding on and what you encounter floating on the lake surface.

5. Early morning is the most productive time. In the afternoons concentrate on windlanes that are formed by steady, moderate breezes because they often carry windblown terrestrials. Evening often sees trout at their most aggressive and they regularly feed the lanes well into the night.

SECTION FIVE

FEEDING PATTERNS

1. TAILING

This describes trout that expose their backs, dorsal fins or tails as they rummage around the bottom in the shallows.

2. PORPOISING

Common when trout are feeding on emergers.

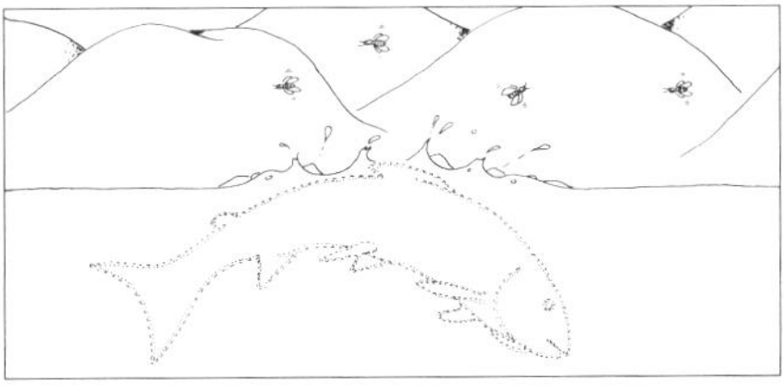

3. SLASHING

Trout are chasing fast moving organisms. Hoppers and snails may also be taken in this fashion.

4. BULGING

Trout are holding just under the surface and tilting upwards to take emergers.

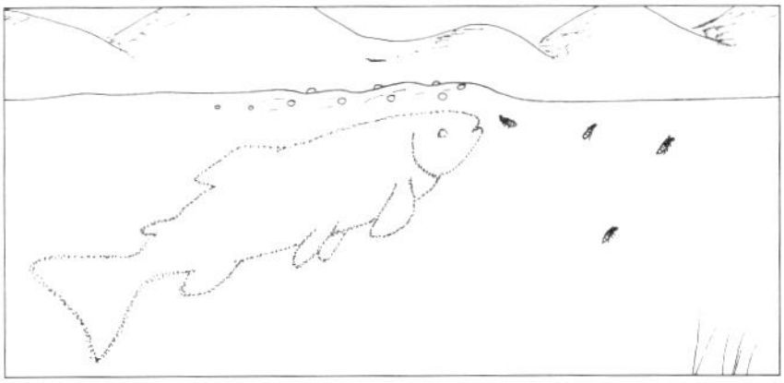

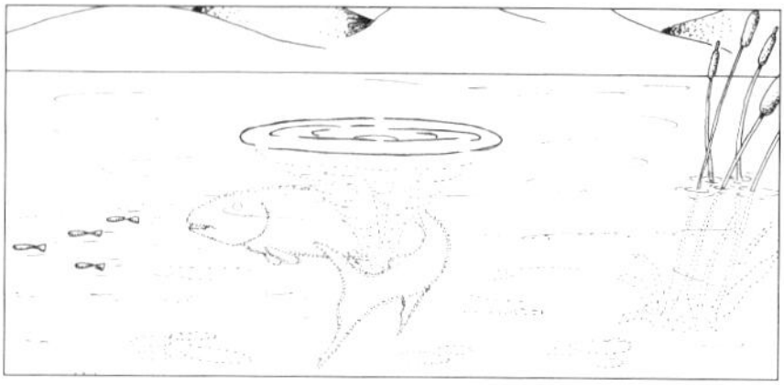

5. SWIRLING

Indicates sub surface feeding.

6. SMALL WHIRLPOOL

Indicates that trout are feeding well below the surface.

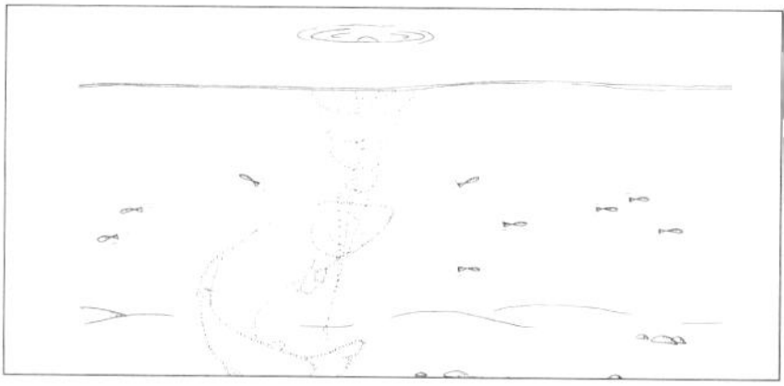

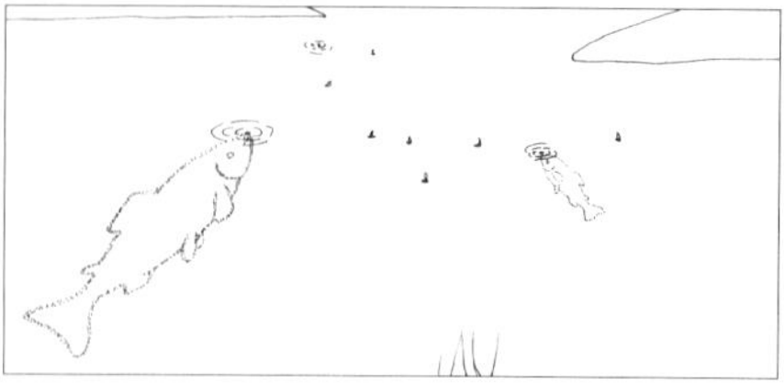

7. SIPPING

Trout are feeding on low riding insects, eg. beetles, ants, spent spinners.

8. NORMAL RISE WITH AIR BUBBLES

Trout are taking insects like mayfly duns off the surface.

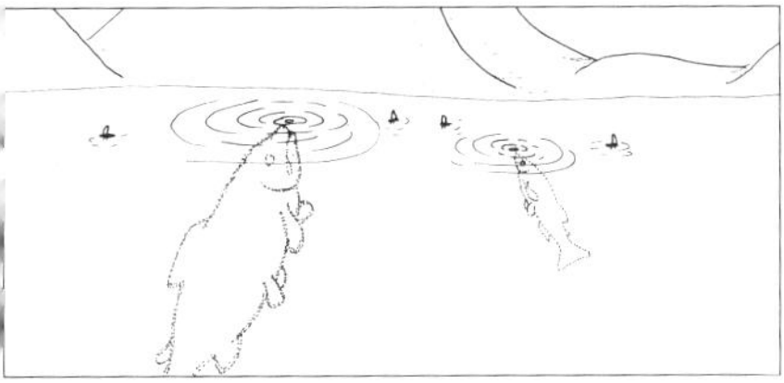

9. NORMAL RISE WITHOUT AIR BUBBLES

Trout are taking emergers just under the surface.

10. LEAPING

Trout are feeding on low flying insects like damselflies, adult caddis or mayfly spinners.

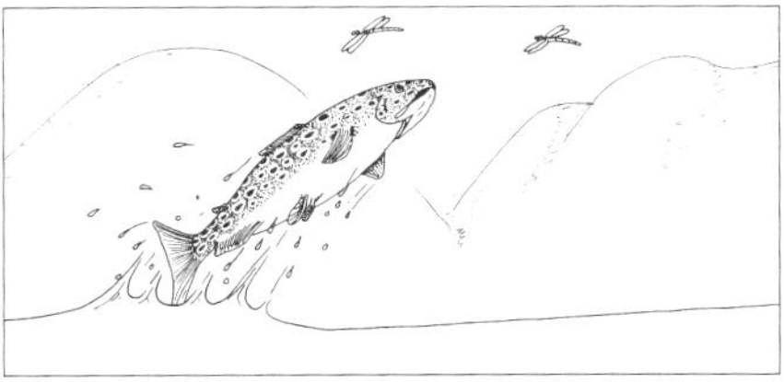

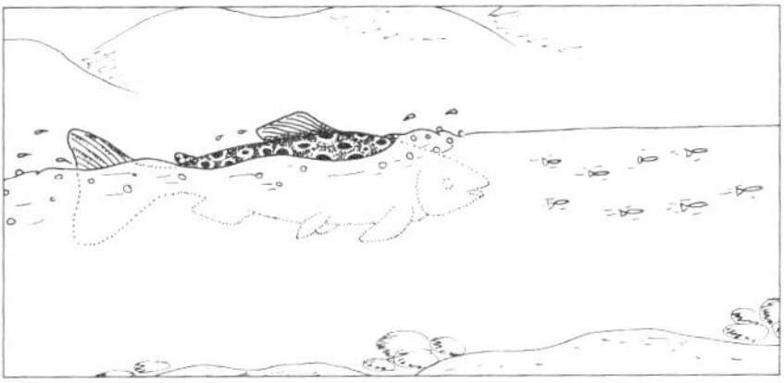

11. SMELTING

This is when trout are targeting small baitfish.

12. NO INDICATION

You are fishing blind and will need to investigate the likely food source or make an informed guess.

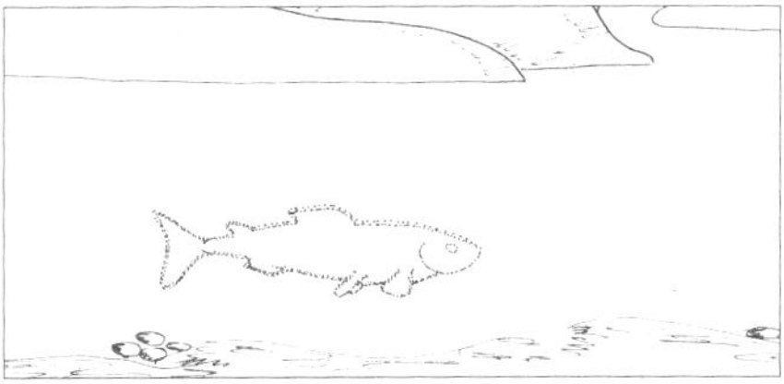

SECTION SIX

TROUT FOODS AND FISHING METHODS

MIDGES

In lakes, Midges are one of the most widely distributed and abundant lake insects. For this reason they are a staple year-round food source for trout.
LIFE CYCLE: Egg, larva (nymph), pupa, adult.

- Nymphs -

Midge larvae range from medium down to minuscule size. They are slow moving, worm-like creatures coloured red, black, grey, yellow, white and various greens and browns.
Where found: Nymphs are found mainly around weedbeds.
Season: All year round.
Feeding patterns: 6,12.
FISHING METHODS
1. NYMPH: Not normally the most productive stage to fish. Best method is to fish a fly slowly along the bottom with an occasional twitch and pause. Maintain a tight line as takes are often gentle.

FLIES: ***Brassie, Bloodworm, Wobble Worm, Godard Red Larva, Kendall Bloodworm, Bucknall Bloodworm, Weighted Fur Nymph.***

- Pupa -

Ascending pupae are poor swimmers and often struggle to break the surface film, making them easy prey.
Where found: Anywhere in the lake.
Time: Anytime. Calm conditions best.
Feeding patterns: Rising pupa 1,2,4,6; emergers 2,7,9.
FISHING METHODS
1. ASCENDING PUPA: Settle the fly on the bottom then commence a slow retrieve with regular pauses. Set the hook at the slightest deviation.
2. EMERGING PUPAE: Grease the leader to within 30 cm of the fly using

5x, 6x tippet. Fish the pattern dead drift or with a slow Figure-8 retrieve. Watch the line closely as takes are usually very gentle.

FLIES: ***Goddard Midge Pupa, Roberts Midge Pupa, Fogg Midge Pupa, Small Seal's Fur Emergers, Buzzer Patterns, Suspender Midge Pupa, Beaver, Black Midge Pupa.***

- Adult Midge -

In the late evening (rarely at morning) mating adults often bunch together forming 'midge balls'. Trout show a preference for these aggregations of food over individual midges.

Where found: Anywhere in the lake.

Time: Anytime. **Feeding patterns:** 3,7,8.

FISHING METHODS

1. MIDGE BALL: Fish the pattern dead drift on a long greased leader with an occasional twitch. For variation, attach a pupa pattern to a 30cm dropper running off the dry fly.

FLIES: ***Griffiths Gnat, Cluster Midge, Midge Ball.***

2. ADULT MIDGE: Dead drift on a long greased leader with an occasional twitch, particularly on cold days when midges take longer to become airborne. A caddis skating technique can also work if the insects are fluttering on surface.

FLIES: ***Polywing Midge, Adams Midge, Knotted Black Midge, Reed Smut, Brown Midge, CDC Adult Midge.***

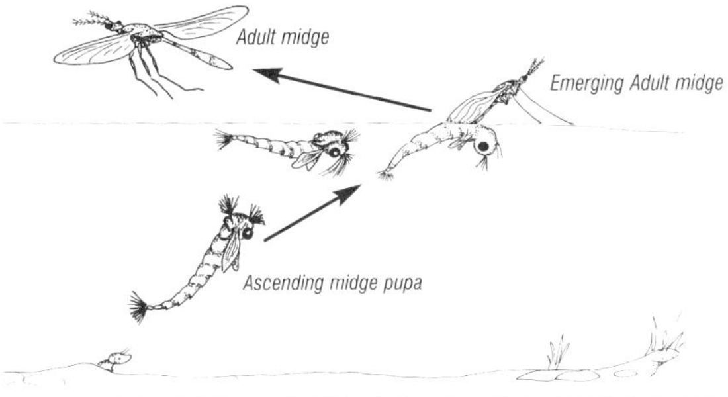

CADDIS

In relatively stable lakes caddis are a primary food source for trout.
LIFE CYCLE: Egg, larva (nymph), pupa, adult.

- Nymphs -

Where found: Nymphs frequent weed beds and vegetation, normally in water not deeper than 3m.
Season: All year round, particularly in winter.
Time: Any time.
Feeding Pattern: Cased nymphs 1,5,6,12; free swimming nymphs 5,6,12.
Crawling cased nymphs construct a protective housing around their bodies from stones and are common around the mouths of cobblestone creeks and rivers flowing into lakes.
Stick caddis nymphs are slow swimmers that construct cases from plant materials and are common throughout a lake.
Free swimming nymphs build no case at all and are free-swimmers.

FISHING METHODS

1. CRAWLING CASED NYMPH: Settle the fly on the bottom, then instigate a dead slow Figure-8 or Hand-twist retrieve with occasional pauses.

> **FLIES:** ***Bead Head Hare's Ear, Hare & Copper, Carrot Nymph, Black & Peacock, Goulburn Caddis, Brassie, Peeking Caddis, Drifting Cased Caddis.***

2. STICK CADDIS NYMPH: Fish the pattern dead drift or with a very slow, slight movement and pauses, just above or next to weeds.

> **FLIES:** ***Murray Wilson Sticky Caddis, Wigram's Stick Caddis, Bailey's Stick Caddis.***

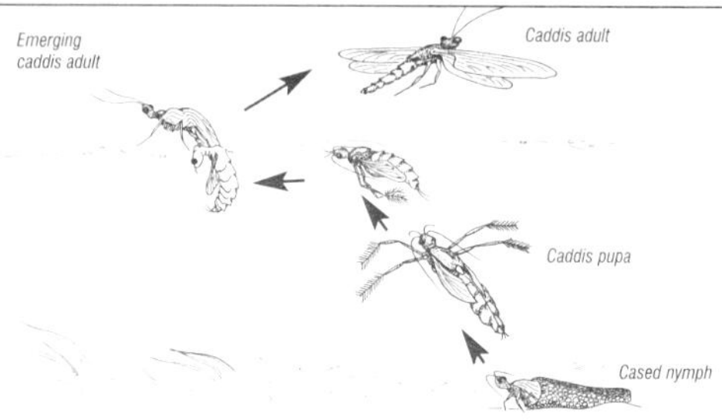

3. FREE SWIMMING NYMPH: Fish the fly dead drift at various depths, or incorporate a gentle rise and fall motion.

FLIES: ***Goulburn Caddis, Olive Caddis Larva, Buckskin Caddis Nymph, Green Rockworm.***

- Pupa -

Where found: The pupa rises to the surface and emerges through the surface film. Pupae are particularly vulnerable and appealing to trout.
Season: Spring through to late summer.
Time: Late afternoon until dark.
Feeding Patterns: 2,4,6,12.

FISHING METHODS

1. RISING PUPA: Cast out and settle the fly on the bottom, then raise it to the surface with an angled, steady retrieve.

FLIES: ***Deep Sparkle Pupa (LaFontaine), or traditional hackle or winged wet flies (March Brown, Invicta).***

2. EMERGING PUPA: Grease the leader to within 30 cm of the fly and fish it dead drift or with a slow Figure-8 retrieve.

FLIES: ***Emergent Sparkle Pupa (LaFontaine), CDC emerger.***

- Adult Caddis -

Season: Spring through to late summer.
Time: Late afternoon until dark and into the night.
Feeding Patterns: 3,8,10.

FISHING METHODS

Adult caddis often flutter across the surface in an attempt to become airborne at such times trout aggressivley try to intercept them before they can leave the water.

1. SLASHING RISES TO ADULT CADDIS: Best fished with a fastish retrieve and rod-lift that skips the fly across the surface.

FLIES: ***Elk Hair Caddis, Goddard Caddis, small Muddler.***

2. SUBTLE RISES TO ADULT CADDIS: Fish the fly dead drift with an occasional twitch.

FLIES: ***CDC Caddis, Senator's Choice or Shannon Moth.***

MAYFLIES

Mayflies are not prevalent in many lakes, but the nymphs are a perennial trout food, and duns can have high seasonal importance.

LIFE CYCLE: Egg, larva (nymph), subimago (dun), imago (spinner).

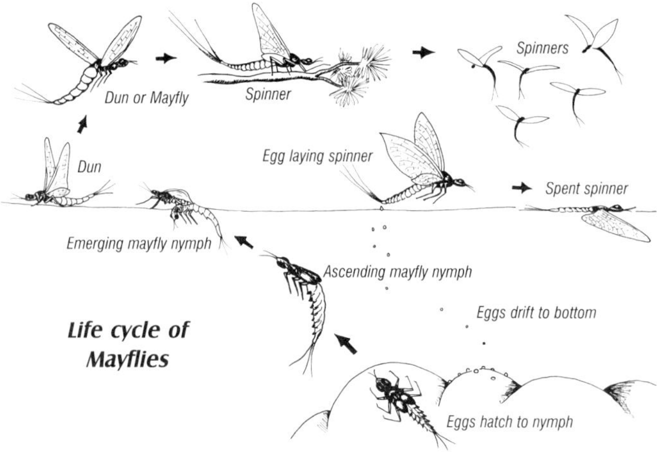

Life cycle of Mayflies

- Nymphs -

The nymphs slowly crawl and dart about the weeds feeding on decaying vegetation, plankton and algae. When they have matured they swim to the surface to emerge. The stop start nature of this ascendancy makes them easy prey.

Where found: Nymphs are common in shallow weed beds.

Season: All year round.

Feeding patterns: Stream-bed nymphs 1,5,6,12; emerging nymphs 4,6; emergers 2,7,9.

FISHING METHODS

1. STREAM-BED NYMPH: In water 30cm to 2m deep fish your fly with a slow Hand-twist or Figure-8 retrieve along the bottom or over the weed, with an occasional twitch and pause. Water 2-3m deep requires a longer leader, or a sinking/sinktip line.

FLIES: ***Pheasant Tail Nymph, Seal's Fur Nymph, Red Fox Squirrel Nymph, Hare & Copper, Baetis Nymph, March Brown, Strip Nymph, Hendrickson Nymph.***

2. RISING NYMPH: Utilise a steadily rising retrieve of an unweighted pattern incorporating a subtle twitch of the rod tip to convey the nymphs halting attempts to reach the surface.

FLIES: ***Pheasant Tail Nymph, Seal's Fur Nymph, Red Fox Squirrel Nymph, Hare & Copper, Baetis Nymph, March Brown, Strip Nymph, Hendrickson Nymph.***

3. EMERGING NYMPH: Grease the leader to within 30 cm of the fly. Dead drift specific emerger patterns, apply floatant to the wingcase area of an unweighted fuzzy nymph, or scissor a dry fly (March Brown etc) hackle down to a stub.

FLIES: ***Cul De Canard, Suspender Nymph, Parachute Brown, Possum, Balloon Emerger, Polywing Emerger, PMD Emerger, Rod's Emerging Dun, Loop Wing Emerger***

- Duns -

Try to match the adult in size and general colour.
Where found: Duns generally shelter along lake margins.
Season: Heaviest in spring.
Time: Mid-morning to mid-afternoon.
Feeding patterns: 8.

FISHING METHODS

1. DUN: Grease the leader to within 30 cm of the fly. If breezy cast upwind of the target area and allow the fly to drift naturally with the wind.

FLIES: ***March Brown, Hardy's Favourite, Highland Dun, Lodge's Dun, Tassie Dun, Greenwell's Glory, Blue Winged Olive, Twilight Beauty, Kosciuszko Dun, Red Quill, Pale Evening Dun, Whirling Dun, Wickham's Fancy, Light Cahill, Quill Gordon.***

- Spinners -

The dun will shed it's exoskeleton to emerge as the often brilliantly coloured spinner. On dusk swarms of these insects will appear along lake margins as they prepare to mate.

Where found: Common along lake margins.

Season: Spring through to late summer.

Time: Calm, warm conditions on dusk are ideal.

Feeding patterns: 7,8.

FISHING METHODS

1. SPINNER: Grease the leader to within 30 cm of the fly on a 5x, 6x tippet. Grease the fly and fish it dead drift with an occasional twitch.

FLIES: ***Macquarie Red, Orange or Black Spinner Patterns, Twilight Beauty, Compara Spinner, Trico Spinner, Quill Gordon, Poly Wing Spinner.***

- Spent Spinner -

After mating, females return to the water to lay their eggs and die. The dead or 'spent' spinner lies flush in the surface film with wings outspread and is keenly taken by trout.

Where found: Spent spinners often accumulate in quiet back waters.

Season: Spring through to late summer.

Time: Dusk and dawn.

Feeding patterns: 4,7,8.

FISHING METHODS

1. SPENT SPINNER: Use an ungreased leader. The wings of the fly should be greased to ensure that the body of the fly is sitting right in the surface film like the natural. Fish it dead drift with an occasional twitch. This low riding fly is difficult to see in the dark so gently strike if you detect a swirl or rise near the presentation.

FLIES: ***Black Spent Spinner, Green Para Drake, Rusty Spinner & Parachute-Hackle or Clipped-Hackle Patterns (Greenwell's Glory, Cocky Spinner, Countless Local Patterns).***

BEETLES

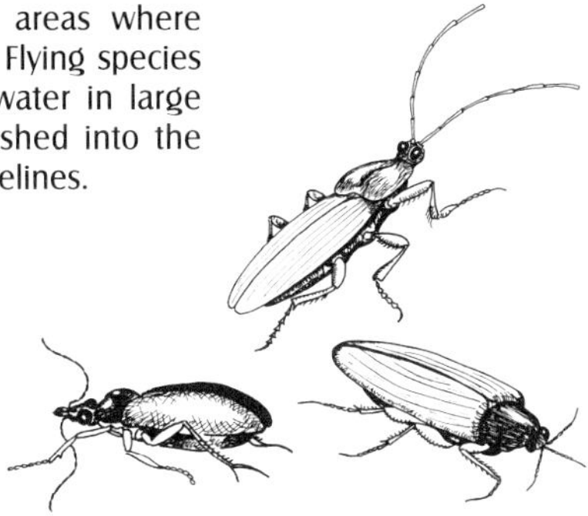

Where found: Common in areas where foliage hangs over the water. Flying species often get blown on to the water in large numbers and are usually washed into the shallows along windward shorelines.

Season: Summer.

Time: All day.

Feeding patterns: 7, 8, 9.

FISHING METHODS

BEETLES: Fish your pattern dead drift or with an occasional twitch. Flies must sit low in the surface film.

FLIES: ***Red Tag, Coch-y-Bondhu, Geehi Beetle, Black and Brown Beetle patterns, Great Lake Beetle, Ti Tree Beetle, Foam Beetle patterns, Jassid, Green Leaf Hopper, Red Palmer.***

ANTS

Ants are on the lake menu occasionally.

LIFE CYCLE: The mating cycle sees ant colonies take to the air over the water in huge swarms. Once mating is completed male ants fall to the water, often in their thousands, to die at which time trout gorge themselves.

Where found: Common around dead trees and rotting timber.

Season: Spring through summer.

Time: Not critical.

Feeding patterns: 7, 8, 9.

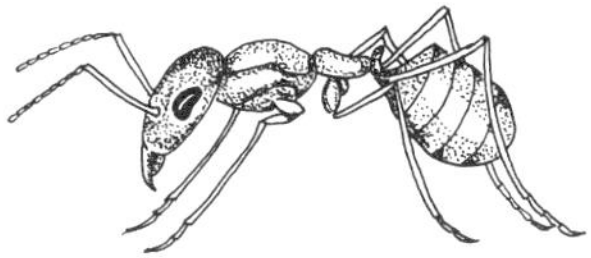

FISHING METHODS

ANTS: Ant flies need to float low in the water to match the naturals. Carry at least two sizes, as trout can be selective. Grease the leader to within 15cm of the fly and fish it dead drift with an occasional slight twitch.

FLIES: Size 12-20 ***Hard Bodied Black Ant, Black Para Ant, Red Fur Flying Ant, E-Z Sight Ant, Black/Red & Grey Ant, Magic Wing Flying Ant, Red McMurray Ant, Rod's Black Ant, Carpenter Ant, Black Deer Hair Ant.***

GRASSHOPPERS

Seek out lakes that have a large, consistently available summer population of grasshoppers.

LIFE CYCLE: The female lays her eggs during winter, hatch in the spring and reach maturity around Christmas.

Where found: Look for long grass that run right up to the water's edge.

Season: Summer through autumn.

Time: Warm afternoons with an offshore wind.

Feeding patterns: 3

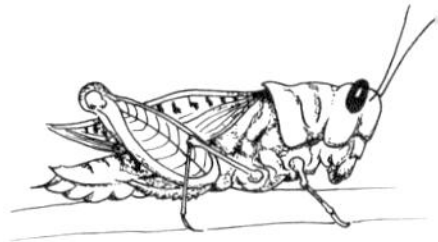

FISHING METHODS

GRASSHOPPERS: Offshore winds blow many hoppers onto the water. In deeper water trout can hold in close to the bank and take these hapless insects with quick, violent strikes.

Smack the fly hard onto the water then incorporate slight twitches to imitate the struggling hopper. Work near the bank first then gradually extend out into the lake.

FLIES: ***Nobby Hopper, Berchdolt, Glen Innes Hopper, Snowy Mountains Hopper, Muddler Hopper, Joe's Hopper, Daves Hopper, Letort Hopper, Whit's Hopper.***

DAMSELFLIES

In warmer months nymphs migrate to shore over fine gravel or mud.

LIFE CYCLE: Egg, nymph, adult.

- Nymph -

Where found: Nymphs live amongst shallow weed beds.

Season: All year round. Emergence occurs during spring to summer.

Time: Usually mid-morning.

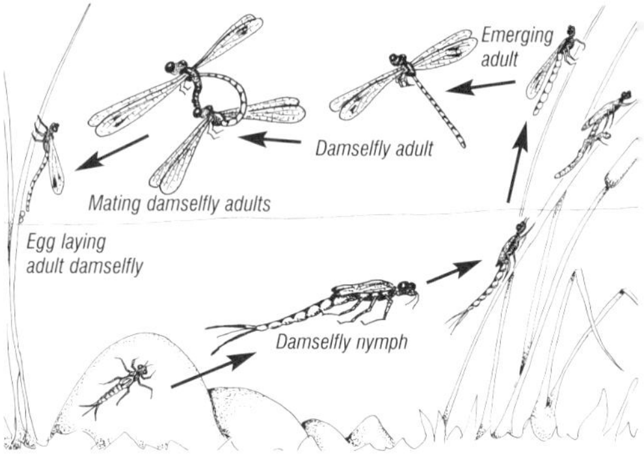

'eeding patterns: Nymphs 1, 2, 4, 12.

ISHING METHODS

NYMPHS: Keep the rod tip close to the water and fish the fly near the)ottom or adjacent to weedbeds, using a series of 2–6mm pulls and pauses vith occasional rod-tip twitches. The take may occur during a pause.

FLIES: ***Marabou Damsel, Green Damsel Fly, Black Damsel Fly, Brown Damsel Fly, Kendall Damsel Nymph, Green Sloans, Long Shanked Green Nymph, Tom Jones.***

- Adult Damselfly -

Adult damselflies are occasionally taken by trout if they end up on the water or are egg-laying. Nymphs are the important food source.

Where found: Lake margins.

Season: Spring through to late summer.

Time: Usually active only on sunny afternoons.

Feeding patterns: 3,8,10.

FISHING METHODS

ADULTS: Drowned adults may be imitated with a Blue or Green Adult Damsel fished dead-drift in the vicinity of feeding fish.

DRAGONFLIES

Dragonflies are rarely taken, but the nymph (mudeye) is a major food.

LIFE CYCLE: Egg, nymph ('MUDEYE'), adult.

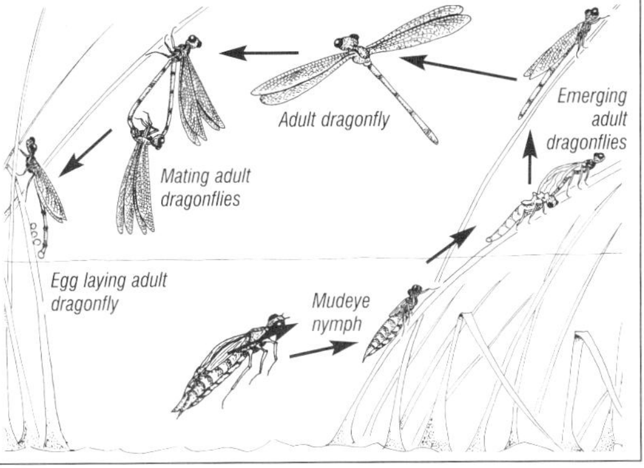

- Nymph -

The mudeye lives in weed and migrates out to the surface to hatch in summer. There are two main species,

the couta and spider.
Where found: Weed beds, sunken timber, rocky areas.
Season: All year, with summer through to Autumn best.
Time: First and last light and through the night.
Feeding patterns: 1,2,4,5,6,9,12.

FISHING METHODS

1. MUDEYES: General searching flies of vague mudeye size and colour, or specific imitations, can be fished slowly just over the bottom with an occasional fast strip and pause. Mass evening/night emergences of spider mudeyes require flies that will sit with their head in the surface film, achieved by using leader grease or fly floatant.

FLIES: ***Craig's Night-Time, Haslem's Bead-Eye Mudeye, Mrs Simpson, Black Muddler, Couta Mudeye, Foam Mudeye Wet, Foam Mudeye Dry, Spider Mudeye Black, Spider Mudeye Brown, Spider Mudeye Green, Cubit's Foam Mudye, Cordulid.***

YABBIES

Yabbies are a major food source in some lakes and feed actively during low light. They move very slowly but flee backwards if threatened.

LIFE CYCLE: Egg, series of adult instars (moults).
Where found: Dark sheltered areas amongst timber and rock.
Season: Most active in summer. Hibernation June-September.
Time: Dawn, dusk and night.
Feeding patterns: 6, 12.

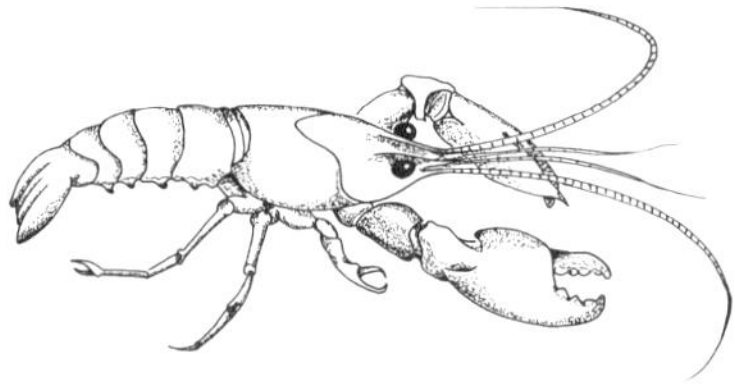

FISHING METHODS

Yabby: Fish slowly along the bottom with a Hand-Twist or Figure-8 retrieve. Deeper water will require a sink-tip line ,long sinking leader, or full-sinking line.

FLIES: ***Brown Yabby, Fuzzy Wuzzy, Whitlock Yabby, Brown Weighted Woolly Bugger, Weighted Yabby, Woolondibby Wonder.***

SNAILS

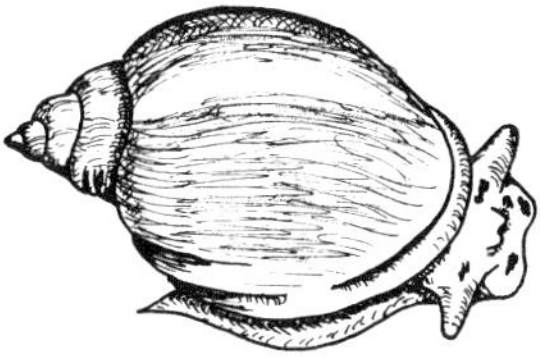

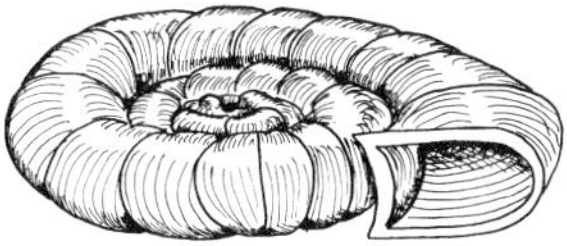

Are rarely found in water more than 3m deep. A productive time to fish snail patterns is after wave action from strong winds has dislodged them, leaving them to float about on the surface.

Where found: Amongst weed beds.

Season: All year.

Time: Anytime.

Feeding patterns: 1, 3, 7, 8, 9, 12.

FISHING METHODS

SNAILS: Fish a pattern dead drift on a greased leader or retrieve very slowly above the weeds.

FLIES: ***Black & Peacock, Wet Coch-y-Bondhu, Snail Fly, Super Snail Fly, Church Snail.***

SCUDS

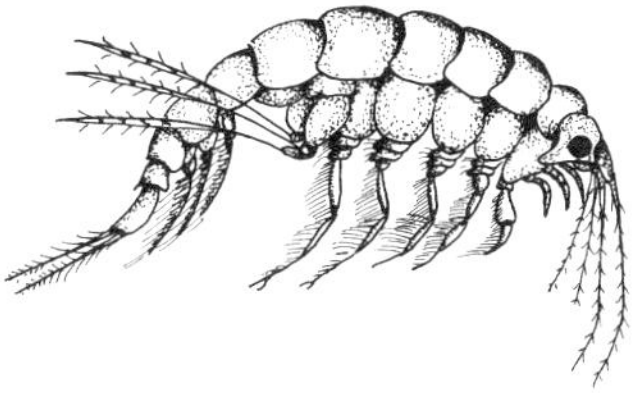

These crustaceans are active in low light conditions and in some lakes are a staple winter diet for trout.

Where found: Scuds are found mostly around weed beds with muddy bottoms in 1-3m of water. They are not as prevalent in lakes that have a constantly fluctuating water level.

Season: All year.

Time: Dawn, dusk and overcast days.

Feeding patterns: 1, 5, 6, 12.

FISHING METHODS

SCUDS: When fishing to tailers, leave the fly inert on the bottom. At other times prospect very slowly with an occasional twitch.

FLIES: ***Small Hare's Ear, Green Nymphs, Scud, Tan Scud.***

SHRIMP

These elongate, largely transparent crustacea normally grow to between 30-35mm in length. Breeding takes place in spring with the eggs hatching in summer.

Where found: Weed beds, sunken boulders and undercut banks along the margins of lowland lakes.

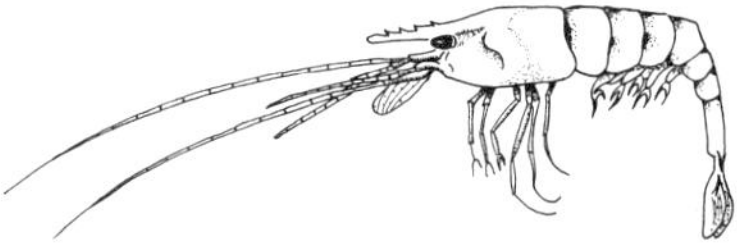

Season: Spring to early autumn.

Time: Low light conditions.

Feeding patterns: 1, 5, 12.

FISHING METHODS

SHRIMP: Foraging shrimp move forward when feeding but dart backwards rapidly when fleeing.

FLIES: ***Shrimp, Black Mountain Shrimp, Olive Monutain Shrimp, Brown Mountain Shrimp, Tom Jones, Slim Green Matuka, Red Spot Shrimp, Goddard Mating Shrimp.***

SMELT

'Smelt' is a term covering several small fish species.

Where found: Smelt normally school for safety in the shallows around weed beds, river mouths, drowned timber and rocky outcrops.

Season: All year. Early to midwinter and early spring are best.

Time: Most active in low light conditions.

Feeding patterns: Watch for schools of smelt jumping out of the water in panic, and/or trout thrashing and crashing about in the shallows.

FISHING METHODS

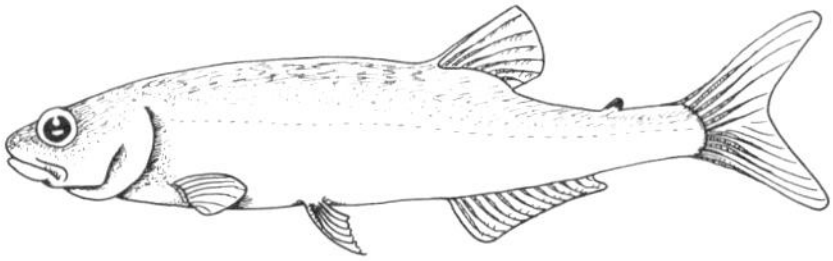

SMELT: Cast in the vicinity of the scattering, panicked minnows then retrieve moderately or with a fast erratic action to imitate a wounded or stunned fish.

FLIES: ***Green Matuka, Tom Jones, Large green nymph ('Big Nymph'), Clouser Minnow.***

LEECHES

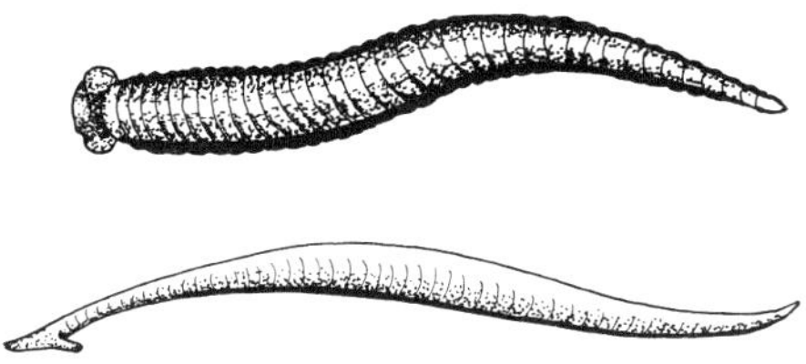

They are not a staple diet for trout but are taken if available.

Where found: Lake shallows with large amounts of rotting vegetation and debris.

Season: All year.

Time: Dawn, dusk & through the night.

Feeding patterns: 1, 6, 12.

FISHING METHODS

LEECH: Fish slowly along the bottom with a rhythmic Figure-8 or Hand-Twist retrieve punctuated with pauses. Move the rod tip up and down to impart an undulating action.

FLIES: ***Marabou Leech (olive, black) and small Woolly Bugger.***

FROGS AND TADPOLES

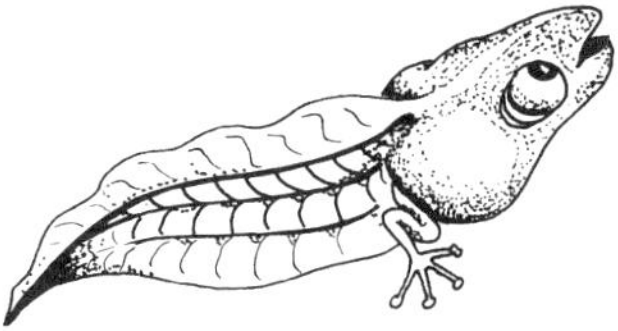

Tadpoles begin turning into frogs within a few days of hatching. Under some circumstances trout will gorge themselves on both.

Where found: Tadpoles school in the shallows along lake margins, look especially in marshy areas with half-submerged rushes.

Season: Spring through summer.

Time: Not critical.

Feeding patterns: Trout thrashing and crashing about in the shallows.

FISHING METHODS

TADPOLES: Trout often charge through schools of tadpoles, then mop up those that are killed or stunned.

Cast your pattern into the feeding zone and retrieve with short, slow, erratic strips to imitate the natural.

FLIES: ***Small Black Matuka, Wigram's Robin, Yeti, Black Fur Fly, Tadpole.***

WATER BOATMEN

Where found: Shallow weedy lake margins not deeper than 1.5 m.
Season: Water boatmen are a common winter food source for trout.
Time: Anytime.
Life cycle: 12 month life cycle from egg to adult. Their shell is normally coloured to match the environment in which they live. By propelling themselves with their oar-like legs, they continually rise to and from the surface to collect air bubbles which they hold against their bodies.
Feeding patterns: 1, 2, 4, 5, 12.
WATERBOATMEN: Wiggle the rod tip to imitate the zig-zag movement of the natural and instigate a moderately fast 2-10 cm stripping action over weedbeds.

FLIES: ***Water Boatman and Backswimmer Imitations are scarce. Black & Peacock, wet Coch-y-Bondhu, Nymbeet or Brown Beetle.***

LEADERS FOR SINKING LINES

Leaders of conventional length sink slower than the flyline and form a belly, causing you to lose full touch with the fly. Fish can take and reject the pattern without you being aware of it. Shortening your leader helps.

SINKING LINE LEADERS

Sinking Line Profile Long/Short Leader

LEADER BALANCE

alancing the mix of 'hard' sections of monofilament with 'soft' ections of monofilament gives anglers the best option for particular shing situations.

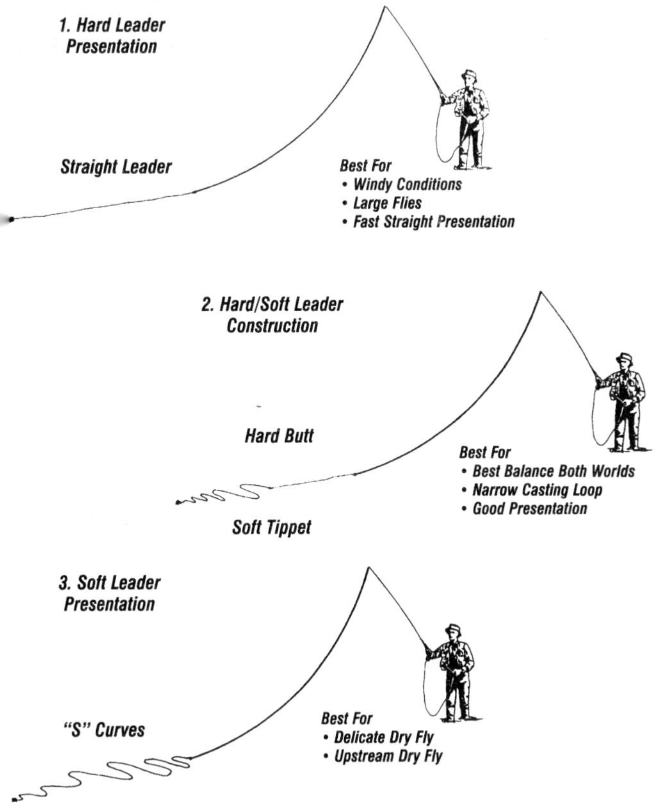

Richard Rule's

Flyfishing Lakes

by Richard Rule
with Rick Keam and Bill Classon

Front Cover Illustration - Based upon David Ashcroft's painting 'Brook Trout on Clarence Lagoon'

Illustrations - Phill Jones

Knots - Geoff Wilson

Design & Production - Dennis Keys

Publishers Bill & Helen Classon

AFN WATERPROOF Pocket Guide No.1

Published and Distributed by Australian Fishing Network

AFN AUSTRALIAN FISHING NETWORK

9 780958 714358

PUBLISHED & DISTRIBUTED BY
Australian Fishing Network
ABN 23 060 058 997
PO Box 544 Croydon,
Victoria 3136, Australia
Ph: (03) 9761 4044
Fax: (03) 9761 4055

ISBN 0-9587143-5-5